From Root to Bloom

Yoga Poems

and Other Writings

By
Danna Faulds

Peaceable Kingdom Books
Greenville, Virginia

ISBN: 978-0-9744106-4-7

Additional copies of this book, and all poetry
books by Danna Faulds
are available by mail.
Send $15.00 (includes postage) to:
Danna Faulds
53 Penny Lane
Greenville VA 24440
The author may be reached by e-mail at
yogapoems@aol.com

Printed in the U.S.A. by
Morris Publishing
3212 East Highway 30
Kearney NE 68847
1-800-650-7888

This book is dedicated to my husband,
Richard Faulds

When I count my blessings,
you are chief among them.
Everything changed from
the day we came together
with such energy, like
magnets, like rockets on
the same unique trajectory,
like two sparks destined to
light one fire in the dark.
My love for you could fill
twenty-seven notebooks
of fine print, every word
true and fresh as that
evening we first met.

Other Poetry Books by Danna Faulds

Go In and In: Poems From the Heart of Yoga (2002)

One Soul: More Poems From the Heart of Yoga (2003)

Prayers to the Infinite: New Yoga Poems (2004)

Danna's poetry also appears in:

Kripalu Yoga: A Guide to Practice On and Off the Mat, by Richard Faulds and the Senior Teachers of Kripalu Center for Yoga and Health (Bantam, 2006)

Sayings of Swami Kripalu: Inspiring Quotes From a Contemporary Yoga Master, edited with introduction and commentary by Richard Faulds.

All books except *Kripalu Yoga: A Guide to Practice On and Off the Mat* are available by e-mailing Danna Faulds at yogapoems@aol.com

Introduction

More and more these days my old orientation is falling away, the needle of my personal compass spinning crazily. Rulebooks and signposts that were helpful in the past don't offer much guidance in this new landscape. The journey into unknown territory reveals all my fears and I have to remind myself often that it also unlocks hidden reservoirs of courage.

To say that we are all traveling a path from the known to the unknown borders on cliché, but I forget every day that this is so. I expect the way to be familiar, the old landmarks comforting, the accustomed routes fulfilling, yet I know deep down that the juice of life only flows when I open myself to what is true in this moment. My life attests to the humbling power of this choice to be present, to turn toward what is here instead of looking away from what I fear, to grow big enough to fully experience reality without the need to hide or stay small.

I look back and shake my head at the amazing series of twists and turns that brought me to this day. "Poet" was not on my short list of possible career choices as a child. In 1962, when I was 10 years old, I watched television with my classmates as John Glenn orbited the earth. The only TV set was in the school basement where we sat on small wooden chairs, the water pipes clanking noisily overhead as a rocket blasted Glenn free of earth's gravity. Something about that sight ignited my own fuse and sent my imagination soaring. I looked up into the blue skies of suburban Long Island that afternoon and proclaimed to my best friend that I was going to be an astronaut.

By the time two Americans walked on the moon seven years later, I had a sense that my ambition wasn't likely to be realized. I hated heights, got claustrophobic in small spaces, and wasn't very good at math or physics. Still, I was riveted to the TV screen that turbulent summer of 1969, following every move Neil Armstrong and Buzz Aldrin made, staring with awe at the footprints they left on the dusty lunar surface. After the astronauts climbed back up the ladder into the lunar module, I walked out to our dark back yard and gazed in wonder at the brilliant moon overhead. They were up there, those two men. Right now they might be looking at the small blue ball of Earth.

Although becoming an astronaut was out of the question, the impetus to explore remained very much alive in me. As it turns out, it was the exploration of *inner* space around which my life was to orbit. My inner journey began in earnest when I discovered yoga in 1983. Its techniques allowed me to reinhabit my body and reestablish a relationship with feelings, sensations, and emotions I had long ago relegated to the shadows. Yoga taught me how to breathe and relax, stretching not just muscles but also expanding me beyond what I thought were the impermeable boundaries of my small self. A potent alchemy occurred when I added a few minutes of free writing to my daily yoga practice in 1990. Writing gave me a way to document my journey as if I were taking word snapshots to describe my varied experiences, and heightened my awareness of yoga's transformative power.

A few years later, I got over my fear of meditation and my journey deepened. Sitting allowed me to hear my harsh self-talk for the first time. Just staying put on the cushion required me to gain the skills needed to watch my mind's relentless machinations closely enough to disentangle from the talons of self-judgment. As I began to actively explore what lay beneath the choppy surface of the mind, I came to realize that what I thought and felt wasn't all of me. Someone was noticing the thoughts and emotions. Who was that?

I took part in my first Enlightenment Intensive in 1999 and discovered that self-inquiry was rocket fuel for me. Three days of contemplating the question "Who am I?" helped me break free of some invisible, gravitational barrier that had always kept me tethered and small. I reached escape velocity that weekend, emerging from the intensive with so much energy that poetry woke me up in the middle of the night for months afterward. While I didn't know it then, the poems that were clamoring to be written would become the backbone of my first book, *Go In and In.*

I am still exploring and still writing. The way from here to there continues to be fascinating. Life keeps tweaking my trajectory, making sure I continue going where I haven't gone before. As I thumb through these newest poems, the attempt to describe my unfolding journey is the thread that holds the pages together. Even the title – *From Root to Bloom* – conveys a sprouting forth from darkness, the slow maturing over time, roots reaching deep, stalk and leaves bringing forth the bud, the flower opening only when it is ready.

At this point in my life, writing serves two primary purposes. Poetry is a natural way for me to reflect on and stay present with what is happening. Whether I'm delving deep inside or observing the natural world, there are countless experiences that draw my attention and beg to be described. I try to write about my actual experience, whether it's falling into the old habit of self-doubt, standing in front of a tombstone and feeling my impermanence, basking in bird song and a joyous sunrise, or facing some sharp edge of inner criticism. Acknowledging both the light and the shadow is important to me, and this book touches on all aspects of my journey over the last two years.

Writing also helps me to discover secrets I am not aware of until they show up at the end of my pen. I often do a practice of free writing in the morning, after meditation or yoga. I write the words

"This is what I have to say to you" at the top of the page, and in the instant that follows, there is a sensation of free-fall in which I have no idea what might come next. Then a phrase leaps into focus, or arises out of nowhere, and my pen begins to race across the page. I write without editing, without even caring if I make sense. Five or ten minutes later, I read over what just emerged, discovering some new part of me that has been revealed or reclaimed. I often have the experience Joan Baez described so vividly: "It seems to me that those songs that have been any good, I have nothing much to do with the writing of them. The words just crawled down my sleeve and came out on the page."

A variety of "trigger phrases" can provide the spark for this kind of writing. "Right now, this is what I know is true" is a good one, or "Today I am here to..." I'll use anything that gets the creative juices flowing and allows me to access the inner connection and sense of wholeness that is too often obscured by my to-do list. Although I tend to combine free writing with other practices, it can be done at any time and in any setting, and requires only a few minutes.

Several days ago, I was trying to meditate while my mind wrestled with the introduction for this book. I had recently chosen the title *From Root to Bloom*, a phrase that suggested a journey, and it was to the question of journeying that my thoughts went back again and again as I attempted to meditate. My mind circled around itself, trying out opening lines and rapidly discarding them. I was getting nowhere when I picked up the pen and began to write:

> This is what I have to say to you. Stop wrestling. Surrender the mind's need to know, the ego's desire to control. You want answers so that you can get on with writing the introduction of your book. "Tell me what the journey is!" you ask, impatient as a five year old stamping her feet. You might as well ask, "Are we there yet?"
>
> Every moment is the journey. You are always in the midst of it, always there, always arriving, always setting out. Your focus on the peak moments or the goal misses the point. Awareness is everywhere. Awareness underlies the most mundane, day-to-day, utterly unremarkable, he-said, she-said, just-burned-the-rice moments. Either you bring awakening with you into every single experience, or you are only half alive.

Surely you see by now that you can't choose your circumstances all the time. No matter what life lays at your feet, that's the journey. And ultimately, what do you have to offer but now, every instant of your life distilled into this instant, everything bringing you right here? Lived with acuity and openness to All That Is, life is unbelievably rich. Miss it because you imagine the real journey is elsewhere, and life feels dry, parched, useless, or confused.

This is it – the journey is everything, and you are in it here and now. Choose to bow to the mystery with humility and gratitude, and you make even more space for truth to enter in.

The power of tapping what lies beneath the surface and letting it bubble out the end of my pen is as effective today as it was the first time I tried it. Once again, the process of writing surprised me. As I read over what I had written, a different thought arose. "Why not include a few of those prose pieces along with my poetry in this new book?" While they could be termed "prose poems," these writings are really the logbook of my inner journey, a more insightful or connected "me" offering myself suggestions for next steps or new ways of looking at old landscapes. They illumine the path from the known to the unknown in a way that is both supportive and a bit confrontational because they tell me the deepest truth I am able to hear (and hence, write) in that moment.

The journey continues, inscrutable, unpredictable, wondrous. I share with you my personal mission statement, hokey though it may be: To live in such a way that I stay open to the vastness and awake to all that is; to be a lover of the mystery and a vehicle for poetry; to serve the whole without needing to know how to go about it.

It has taken me a while, but I now find it liberating that I can't know in advance how to do anything that is mine to do in this life. I really don't know how to offer you these writings, but I'm doing it anyway, grateful for your interest in the journey we all share, inviting you inside my little slice of life. Thanks for your support.

Danna Spitzform Faulds
July, 2006

Acknowledgements

A number of teachers and spiritual friends have made significant contributions to my journey over the last two years. Thanks to Yogi Amrit Desai (Gurudev), his wife Urmila (Mataji), and son Malay, Mickey Singer, Adyashanti, and the sisters of the Abbey of Regina Laudis. Each of them opened doors for me that proved to be important.

Adele and Justin Morreale embody good heartedness and generosity. Our growing friendship means so much.

I am grateful for the support and inspiration of fellow poets David Bryant, Guy Kettelhack, and Paul Weiss. To special friends who were always there with a kind word or a perfectly timed e-mail: Margaret Klapperich, Kathy Kuser, and Marc Paul Volavka – I couldn't have written these poems without you.

To my colleagues at Kripalu Center and the Woodrow Wilson Presidential Library, particularly Jessica Atcheson, Grace Welker, Heidi Hackford, and Rick Potter, I can't thank you enough for your flexibility, understanding, and good humor.

Friends and family have reached out in very tangible ways to support my writing and love me no matter what: Tara Brach, George and Mary Lou Buck, Sister Cecilia, Stephen Cope, Ida Cullen, Andre and Jo-Anne D'Alfonso, John and Kay Faulds, Sudhir Jonathan Foust, Gay Gill, Ann Greene, Martha Harris, Jackie Kaufman, Lloyd Klapperich, Atma Jo Ann Levitt, Vandita Kate Marchesiello, Lawrence Noyes, Len and Ling Poliandro, Nadia Puttini, Marc and Meryl Rudin, Bill and Lila Schafer, Patricia Smail, Heather and Logan Ward, and the Spitzform clan, Hal, Marianne, and Peter.

To all you yoga teachers sharing your gifts with such dedication, my respect knows no bounds. That you read my poetry in your classes touches me more than I can say. Thank you for all you offer the world, and for making this book of poetry possible.

Special thanks to Ila and Dinabandhu Sarley for the personal sacrifices they are making to lead the evolving expression of Kripalu Center

On the occasion of his retirement, I thank Michael Kline, my former college French professor, who taught me to see the world in new ways, to look beneath the surface, and to appreciate the astonishing power of words.

I gratefully acknowledge the memory of William Meneely, whose life and love continues to echo in my heart a decade after his death.

To my husband, Richard, the most truthful, rigorous, and compassionate editor I can imagine, your willingness to listen as I read each day's passel of poetry or prose has helped my confidence to grow. Your choice to share your own insights and learnings, to articulate the cutting edge of your journey is constantly stimulating and inspiring me to try new directions.

And to anyone missed in the hustle and bustle of doing the needful to get this book to press, thanks be to you too.

Awareness Knowing Itself

Settle in the here and now.
Reach down into the center
where the world is not spinning
and drink this holy peace.

Feel relief flood into every
cell. Nothing to do. Nothing
to be but what you are already.
Nothing to receive but what
flows effortlessly from the
mystery into form.

Nothing to run from or run
toward. Just this breath,
awareness knowing itself as
embodiment. Just this breath,
awareness waking up to truth.

Erasing the Line

The pagan priestess of my soul
already knows many answers.
She leans out over the waters
of life and peers beneath the waves.
She sees what I have been afraid
to see – the snaky eels hiding in
the shadows, the nameless creatures
that never rise to the realm of light.
The wild, Druid heart of me looks
from my eyes with courage I didn't
know was there, with willingness
to be temptress, crone, slayer of
fears, or holy fool. Banishing
nothing from her sight, she
witnesses the dark side. This is
how I grow, receiving in
awareness what was exiled
long ago, letting truth in, daring
to be whole and human, whole
and divine, erasing the line
between what I dare to know
and what I must keep hidden.

Yoga's Reach

It is a wonder
how a simple stretch
deepens breath,
and an elegantly held pose
grows to touch the
whole of me.

Like sugar stirred into tea,
the potency
of yoga spreads
from body into mind
and heart, revealing
an ocean of energy
that heals and opens,

holds me close
and sets me free
all in the same moment.

My Point of View

My point of view is not
a fixed or singular thing.
To say "I am the body,"
or "I am the vastness" –
both are true, and neither.

To be all of it at once is to
fling my arms wide under
the shining sun and shout
"yes" with all my strength,
but even then I am not done.

Beneath the all and
everything I've just
embraced is the great,
unchanging silence, the
emptiness from which
the multiplicity arises.

To let my "yes" encompass
even this annihilates all
labels, takes away the
ground beneath my feet, and
leaves me perilously free.

Circle of Breath

Inhale and let go.
Over and over,
the circle of breath
brings me into
this moment.

The even flow of air,
the act of taking in
and giving back,
breathing draws me
inside the radiant
reality of now.

I can't breathe deeply
and be fearful, breathe
freely and be anywhere
but here, the whole
of me embodied in these
waves of breath.

Maybe Not

Begin somewhere.

Take one deep breath
and dive.

Plunge into the core
of your most
persistent fear,
or your greatest joy.

Grow comfortable
with the act of
exploration.

Well, maybe not
comfortable,
but confident of
your ability to be
sure footed
on slick rocks,
steady while the
winds gust.

Well, maybe not
entirely confident,
but willing to set out
despite persistent
doubts, breathing
your way into
whatever you are facing.

Well, maybe not even
all that willing,
but you take it
anyway, that first step
into the unknown.

Courage is starting
where there is
no secure outcome,
no sure result.

The secret is you can
begin again at any time.

Take one deep breath,
and dive.

Ready to Let Go

It isn't really difficult,
this bridging of the realms.
It takes no special agility,
no training in firewalking
or turning cartwheels on
a tightrope, just a blend
of will and surrender.

When I open to the source
of wonder, I let go of the
trapeze to soar weightless
and amazed. I calculate
without thinking, and grab
the next trapeze bar on the fly.

Will and surrender are not
adversaries but two ends of
one broad arc that fills the
circus tent with life.
There can be no show
unless the acrobat
is ready to let go.

Nest Building

I watch a crow land
in the dogwood, hopping
here and there, carefully
scrutinizing each branch.

Then the strong beak
slices through a twig,
and the bird is an ebony
arrow flying for the pines,
off to weave the pliant stick
into its nest.

I daydream of crow eggs
hatched in a cradle of
dogwood blooms, white
blossoms soothing the
bird brood, all beak and
fluff, awaiting the arrival
of the black winged
goddess bearing food.

After the High

After the high, after the
peak experience when I
knew myself as everything
and nothing, when I saw
through body-mind as if
my eyes were x-rays that
pealed away identity and
masks, after the expansion
came the crash. Issues
reappeared, and my
humanness embarrassed
me at every turn. Doubt
emerged to lead a parade
of difficult emotions.

I wanted peace, tranquility,
and bliss, not this mundane
sludge spilling out to muddy
my clear waters. It took a
long time to tune my focus
not to absent bliss but to the
minute examination of the
mud. As I dove into the
most ingrained habits and
the darkest of my fears,
that's when things began
to shift. That's when freedom
ceased to be mere concept
and I began to understand
the power of self-observation
without judgment.

The Kingdom of Worms

I forget from year to year how
thunder rumbles, echoes, bounces
from mountain to mountain. I forget
how it shakes the house, vibrations
moving through beams and floor
boards. I forget how lightning
surprises with a flash, how fat drops
sound like hail.

In a lull between two downpours
cardinals sing triumphantly. If it were
me I'd undoubtedly complain, but not
the mockingbird who serenades,
not the chickadee, even when the rain
begins again. And in the midst of this,
a robin proclaims for every ear to hear,
"The kingdom of worms is before us today.
Rejoice now, and be grateful."

Every Step is Holy

The journey from known
to unknown, from the
unreal to the real, is rarely
revealed in advance.
The potholes, detours,
false starts, and quick
retreats are each honorable,
and even needed in the bigger
scheme, in the forest that can't
be seen between the trees.

It took years for me to realize
that the very twists and turns
and shadows I labeled "problems"
were really sacred ground,
grace disguised as obstacles,
the whole path a pilgrimage,
mysteries baring themselves
before me all along the way.

On the Other Side

I put all of my conditioning aside
for one glorious instant and slide
through the eye of the needle,
threading it with light. On the
other side there is no portal
for return, but I don't even
think about that. Cutting the
cord, I dance as I never dared in
that other world, dance as if I
am loosed from gravity and
delivered into the arms of
jubilation. Reveling, merging,
spiraling inward or out, down
or up, alive and wild, I am
freed even from what I believed
freedom would be.

Life Breathes Me

It sometimes feels like
leaping off a cliff simply
to stay present with
what is. Practice shifts
and shapes me, shaves
off my roughest edges,
illumines the dark places.
As my focus of awareness
shifts, life breathes me,
and energy is freed to
heal even the most
hopeless rifts.

This is what I have to say to you. In the first stage of your journey you learned to replace harmful beliefs with helpful ones. It was such a relief to let go of negativity that it became a temptation to stay there – to make your home in those newly acquired positive thoughts. But a positive self image is still a mask. The next stage of your journey is becoming comfortable with the unknown. It involves being clear and courageous enough to rest in bare awareness without having to create another identity, without needing to tack yet another belief to the end of "I am."

Experience the expansion, the spaciousness that comes from resting in the truth of unknowing. It isn't comfortable, at least not now, but it is powerful and inherently creative. It's what your soul longs for. Use the sense of vertigo to leave behind the known, and let go of the need to tether your soul to anything solid or definable. Let yourself go, over and over, until it is second nature to be weightless.

The Open Door

A door opens. Maybe I've
been standing here shuffling
my weight from foot to foot
for decades, or maybe I only
knocked once. In truth, it
doesn't matter. A door opens
and I walk through without a
backward glance. This is it,
then, one moment of truth in
a lifetime of truth; a choice
made, a path taken, the
gravitational pull of Spirit
too compelling to ignore any
longer. I am received by
something far too vast to see.
It has roots in antiquity but
speaks clearly in the present
tense. "Be," the vastness says.
"Be without adverbs, descriptors,
or qualities. Be so alive that
awareness bares itself
uncloaked and unadorned.
Then go forth to give what you
alone can give, awake to love
and suffering, unburdened by
the weight of expectations.
Go forth to see and be seen,
blossoming, always blossoming
into your magnificence."

Quiet Revolution

Mine is a quiet revolution.
No fireworks light the sky
proclaiming liberation, just
the sure sense of presence
filling me with stillness.
I can't seem to worry
anymore, can't make myself
rush to finish what I once
deemed so important. Instead,
I stand awestruck before the
sunrise, grateful for another
day to love and be loved –
so simple and so humbling.

Moon Shadows

Just now the moon broke through,
casting ghostly shadows on our path.
Darkness dispelled, we could have
read an eye chart or a map marked
with an arrow, "You Are Here."
And it's true, we *are* here, sniffing
the scent of thawing ground on this
nearly spring night, striding through
puddles of moonlight. Then, quickly
as the moon had come, it simply
slipped away. The sky sewed the
only cloud-hole closed, drawing
the edges in until they neatly
overlapped. The moon's face
disappeared, leaving the clouds
to glow as if a weary seamstress
labored late, hands guided by
a candle flame.

When the Desert Blooms

Yearning, deep as dry roots
reach, wide as desert sky,
yearning is my entry point.
Like thirst that can't be
quenched, or hunger for some
sacred food not grown in
any soil, only communion
will do. Only intimacy with
you, only the direct route,
my heart to yours, will cause
this cactus flower to bloom.

All the good intentions in
the world and still I cease
to see, forget divinity, lose
sight of why I'm here until
yearning rouses me again,
and brings me back to praying
in the sand. Tears leave
streaks beneath my eyes,
run into the cracked and
dusty corners of my mouth.
In my raw, unvarnished need,
I feel your presence, known
and flowing like the headwaters
of life. You wash me clean
of my forgetting.

Ten Breaths

I count out ten deep
breaths before I enter
the adventure of my
practice, ten breaths
to bring myself present
in the here and now.
Ignited by awareness,
energy wakes and
carries me from effort
into ease. Presence
itself breathes through
me, the unseen
substance of love so
tangible and strong
that each long breath
offers up the key
to my release.

Inside the Bull's Eye

From the moment we are old
enough to listen, we receive
instructions to improve our aim,
buy better arrows, refine the
grip of fingers on bow string.
Think of the irony. Here we sit
within the bull's eye, aiming
at externals.

The good news is that every
practice done with love and focus
eventually reveals the insanity of
targeting a distant goal. By
then we've grown so used to
holding the bow, drawing the
string back with just the right
amount of force, that it's hard to
put the arrow down and just be
present in the bull's eye.

Perfect Emanation

The perfect emanation is
alive inside each one of us
right now. I'm not denying
my imperfect translation,
my stumbling fits and starts,
or my dark side.

Yet look at what is
manifesting! Witness how
the thread comes off
the spool without tangles,
how the tapestry of life
weaves itself,
using me as loom.

Posture of Divinity

I reach inside the stretch
to remember again
the infinite being that is
beyond individual identity –

the ageless, wise and
joyful one, awareness
released from expectation
or the need to understand.

I find the alignment
of soul and breath,
the perfect line
of consciousness.

In the center of my movement,
nothing is left of me
but what is true and intimate –
the posture of divinity.

Truth Is Infinite

I shift from light
to dark, from fear
to knowing, from
separate to whole
and back again a
thousand times
each day, but truth
is patient. It waits,
undiminished by
my circumstances,
not wavering even a
fraction of a degree
from reality. Truth
waits until I wake,
until I leave my
forgetfulness behind,
until I gather all my
courage and look
inside. Fear only
seems bottomless;
truth is infinite.

Mother of the Universe

Holy mother of the universe,
some inner compass knows
that you exist, and points
to the kiss of sun on crocus.

I kneel to touch their loveliness,
those colorful explosions of
hope amidst the cold. Crouched
there, heart beating near the
earth, I sense you pouring life
force into everything, holding
a vessel that is always full.

Holy mother of the universe,
you who offer sustenance and love,
give life to buds, and turn winter
into spring, I turn my face in your
direction. Drinking, I am filled.

Epitaph

A few words deftly carved
in marble,
names and dates,
the outline of a life
reduced to these etched phrases.

A ladybug carries her curved and
speckled shell
into the gully of the letter C
and out the other side,
crawling left to right across
first name, middle, last,
reading a biography in Braille.

Reaching the edge of the headstone
she spreads her wings,
launches into the canopy
of newly opened oak leaves,
and vanishes in sunlight.

Wholeness

I dive inside a reservoir
of darkness and find my
luminous heart pulsing
like a star. Illusions divide,
take sides, tell me I will
always dwell in light or
shadow. Truth unifies,
casts aside barriers, frees
me from polarities. When
I slip beneath the surface
there is only one energy
flowing from the vastness
into form. It manifests as
opposites, masquerades
in such a convincing way
that I forget from day to
day that there is just a
single source. Seeing past
truth's masks, I rest
at last in wholeness.

Buoyancy

I've regained a natural buoyancy,
as if the spirit in me just won't stay
down for long.

It still surprises me to be the witness of
these moods. Overnight I shift from sad
and brooding to joyous. In one day I may
feel grief, contentment, anger,
ease, and bliss.

Feelings lift and lower like a rowboat on
the waves. I am neither the stories I tell
myself nor the emotions that
accompany the tales.

I am the one who witnesses,
who sees the spider spin her web
without getting caught
in the sticky threads.

This is what I have to say to you. Do not let the day slip through your fingers, but live it fully, now, this breath, this glimpse of newly risen sun catapulting you into full awareness. Time is precious, minutes disappearing like water into sand unless you choose to pay attention.

Since you do not know the number of your days, treat each as if it is your last. Be that compassionate with yourself, that open and loving to others, that determined to give what is yours to give, and to let in the energy and wonder of this world.

If you are tempted by complacency to miss the gift of twin fawns in the yard, or a towhee scratching at the feeder, choose to be awake instead. Experience everything – writing, relating, eating, doing all the necessary little tasks of life – as if for the first time, pushing nothing aside as unimportant.

You have received these same instructions many times before. This time take them into your soul, for if you choose to live this way, you will be rich beyond measure, grateful beyond words, and the day of your death will arrive with no regrets.

From Root to Bloom

Sap is flowing once again
from root to trunk, from
trunk to branch, to every
leaf and bud and blossom
on the tree. The frozen days
are past. Now is the season
of flowering, when the full
force of energy moves up and
up to manifest its destiny.

It is everything to me, this
new life springing forth from
ash and compost, this chance
to nurture, weed, and prune,
to patiently receive the
miracle that blooms as if
no force on earth can
turn aside its beauty.

Initiation

Poised on a precipice,
I know I am ready.
Fall or fly, the time
is ripe to make the
leap. I deepen my
breath, noting both
anxiety and excitement.

Stepping off the edge,
I cannot predict what
comes next. Aware of
everything at once,
I am uncertain if I
flew or I was carried,
but when I find myself
in entirely new territory,
I realize life will never
be the same again on
this side of my initiation.

There Is Love Here

I feel the warm
embrace of spirit
flowing into me
from somewhere
I can't see. There
is love here, arising
inside me as naturally
as the sky brightens
before dawn – love
enough to fill all of us,
and more besides.
The spontaneous grace
of the divine is moving
through the universe,
unfazed by fear or
obstacles of any kind.
Yes, it's clear
there is love here.

Surrender Is Everything

"Surrender is everything," he said
to me as we walked one foggy
evening on the lane.

I tried it, letting go, allowing truth
to swallow me whole, digest me, spit me
out again. I tried it, releasing my tight
grip on mind and what I thought my
world should look like. Life flowed
into me then, astonishingly fresh.
I came alive in ways I couldn't have
guessed, experiencing life as if I was
a newly opened blossom.

"Yes," I said the next night as we
walked. "Surrender is everything."

Resurrection

Yesterday a warbler flew into
the sliding door and died.
There was the sharp rap
of beak on glass, a dull thud,
then nothing.

I saw the body several times,
and felt a stab of guilt.
If only we hadn't built the
house, if only the light
had been different.

If, if, if – my sadness
offered nothing to the bird
lying so still, its lifeless eyes
gazing up and up.

At first light I looked again,
expecting the chill of regret,
expecting the thought,
"Today I must bury that bird."

Instead, I saw only
the flat stones of the patio,
new weeds poking through
the cracks.

Did a fox come in the night,
a few scant feet from where
I slept? Did the rapture arrive,
and I was left behind?

Did the bird recognize with
a flutter of wings that death
wasn't what it feared?

Did it rise and rise,
this small patch of earth
growing smaller,
everything falling away?

My Authentic Voice

I know my authentic voice
because it moves me like
no other. Emerging not from
the grooves of habit or belief,
but out of far left field,
or wherever the mystery
resides in me, it surprises
with honesty or shocks me
out of my complacency.

From the babble of competing
voices in my head, this one
stands out. I know my authentic
voice because integrity insists
on being noticed. It delivers
the experience of truth, the
take-my-breath-away instant
when presence fills every
cell of me with "Yes."

Silver Lining

Fog paints everything
with the same gray
brush. The contours
of the woods are
obscured in mist,
the tops of pine trees
nearly hidden. On the
window screen, drops
of water sit within the
mesh where they
collected overnight,
growing like crystals
in the damp breeze
blowing from the
east. It is like waking
in a cloud, the silver
lining etched on every
spider's web, haze
shrouding nature's
secrets until a pale
sun lifts the veil to
reveal the world in
all its dripping glory.

Pot of Gold

Here, before a crowd of cloud witnesses
I give you this blessing:

Borrow my faith until your own grows
strong enough to bear your weight.

Borrow my gratitude until you awaken
from your slumbering depression to
hear the song of wind and sky
with your own ears.

Borrow my appreciation for life even
if your own delight is dim or nonexistent. Borrow my eyes so you can
see beauty as I do.

For a time, borrow my thoughts and set
your doubts aside. Borrow light, which of
course isn't mine, residing as it does
in all of us.

What good is energy if I can't lend mine
when yours is spent? This isn't weakness
or charity, this isn't dependence, but
simply sharing an abundance of love.
Here, for the asking, is not just the
pot of gold, but the rainbow.

Borrow it until you can spin your own
gold out of nothing, until violet and
yellow and all the spectrum's colors
arrive to keep you company again,
until you hold an artist's palette
that clamors to be shared.

First Light

At first light I am received in love,
as if the Mystery waited patiently
for my emergence out of sleep.
For just a moment there are no
responsibilities to shoulder, just
the soft and spreading glow of dawn,
possibilities unfolding before me like
buds beneath the sun.

Yes, there are choices to be made in
every moment of this day; choices
between acceptance and judgment,
fear or love. Life isn't about
vanquishing one to claim the other,
but being present with their totality
and sum, excluding none.

When the Bubble Bursts

Active mind seeks answers,
quiet mind embraces silence.
Beneath both, thoughts
float like soap bubbles.

Iridescence rises for a moment,
then bursts,
leaving nothing in its wake
but open space.

Your True Name

Listen. The Beloved
is singing you a
love song.

Right now, as you
sit inside your house
of bone and flesh,
the Beloved knows
your essence.

Do you hear the
subtle sound of
breath, the bullfrog
chorus borne upon
the wind? Do you
experience the
silence beneath
the hummingbird's
quick wings?

The Beloved never
stops speaking
your true name.

Dare to be Nothing

Sit in the space
that exists before
you try to meditate.

Rest in the quiet
that underlies all
thought.

Return again and
again to flowing
stillness without
denying a single
expression of truth.

Dare to be nothing,
know nothing,
do nothing, until the
vastness pours
through you.

Live the absolute
behind the relative,
the unifying love
beneath all
points of view.

Earth's Own Congregation

I am received by earth's own
congregation into a green
sanctuary with no need of
walls or vaulted ceiling.

Embodied spirit celebrates
rebirth, each creature offering
its uniqueness to the whole.

How can I possibly feel separate
when nature dances with me
on the grass – the nodding tulips
and small azure moths, the wood
thrush, clouds, and groundhog.

The snorting doe who stomps
her hoof upon the ground, and the
swaying pine boughs, they all
know Easter's secret –

the wondrous, freeing peace of
the risen sun, the blooming bud,
the heart laid bare with love and
wonder, the many joined as one.

This is what I have to say to you. Don't manage fear, but plunge right in its midst. Feel the gut clench, jaw set, shoulders stapling themselves to your ears. Acknowledge the weariness with life, the dreary, plodding, "enough already" of it.

It feels like you could die inside this fear, and so you must. Die to past and future, right and wrong. Die to approval-seeking and the need to know anything except this moment. Die to your desire to be safe, secure, and sure that the future will roll out in your control.

You need not do anything concrete to allow these things to die. Just be. Put no object or subject with the verb. Present to your most essential self, naked and untamed, outside the frame of mind or time, just be.

You'd think this would be easy, but if you actually witness the dizzying antics of the mind, it wants everything but this open-endedness. It thinks up nonexistent problems just to solve them. It insists on change, or self-expression, or anything but just sitting in the moment as it is.

Stripped bare, awareness shines like a beacon in the night. I say live in that light today. Let action flow naturally from your connection to reality, neither banishing the mind, nor bowing to it as your master. Just be and receive everything the present reveals with equanimity. You are ready!

Hope and Innocence

Rain pours down the open
throats of lilies, into the
upturned mouths of pink
petunias. The same rain
knocked down the sunflower
planted in our garden by
the birds. It lies dying,
its round face in the mint
leaves as if to sniff their sweet
fragrance and lend its golden
color to the green. A wet buck
deer appears at the salt lick,
all ears and velvet antlers,
peering into the mist.
This is why I live out here,
far from the conveniences
of town. The storm-cleansed
garden and the two small
fawns who clown around
at the border of our woods
remind me that despite the
state the world is in, there is
still hope and innocence.

Time Enough

The wisdom voice says:
"Be still. Take time for
what is truly important."

I imagine myself diving,
leaving behind an untidy
trail of what's not needed.

I cast aside worry,
which has never brought me
anything even remotely useful.

I let go of doubt, and all the
countless ways I tie myself
in knots.

Scattered behind me like
discarded clothes are
old beliefs, selfish agendas,
my fixed and false identities,
attachment to particular results.

Weightless, and miraculously
free, my eyes shine
with wonder and enthusiasm.

The wisdom voice says:
"There is always time enough
for joy."

Bright Day

The hill of daffodils
shines like the sun
come down to drink
its fill of light.
Spring unrolls its
leafy carpet, the
whole world going
green, reminding
me that miracles are
not just vague
possibilities, but real
as mockingbird
melodies, obvious as
dewdrops flashing like
prisms in the grass.

Inner Demon

The black hole of my self-
loathing lets no ray of light
escape. It waits in shadow,
outside the reach of
conscious thought. Then
when old emotions strip
me bare, in a vulnerable
moment, self-loathing roars
to life, an uncaged, mythic
monster spreading darkness.

My sunny disposition
disappears, and optimism
turns to dust. The only way
out is through the heart of
my despair, daring to feel
the dense and suffocating
negativity spread like an
infection. Even caught in
this bad dream, something
beyond the silent scream
bears witness. The me of me
is unaffected by the poison.
It takes whatever time it
takes to turn and face my
desperate inner demon and
love it back to light.

Yoga Doing You

Let postures flow,
movement as natural
as moonrise,
being without doing.

Go right to the edge,
to the spark within
each breath, and inquire
into the awareness that
underlies the stretch.

Release the small me
clamoring to be seen,
and experience the
emptiness beneath,
the boundaryless
expanse of freedom.

This leap outside a
fixed identity,
this free fall into truth
is, very simply,
yoga doing you.

Love Song

I thought I knew you,
but as I lose myself
inside your eyes,
I am content to know nothing.

I thought you knew me,
but now you look right
through my identity.

I thought we understood
each other, and we do,
but only in that place
where love flows in from
the mystery,
where form and emptiness
dance, and our hands
join without grasping.

We meet and part and meet
again, each time fresh,
the slate wiped so clean
there is no slate,
no hook to hang our hats on.

Each morning we say yes,
our gaze holding only wonder.

Gospel of Reality

I am open space as wide
as all creation. Indefinable,
untamed, bearing no name,
I am the knower of senses
and embodiment. I breathe
life into the dirt, the earth,
the sky and stars, the first
creative impulse of the artist.

Light and darkness are
both part of me, yes and no,
matter flowing in from
the unknown. I am energy
and attention, the source,
the matrix, and the womb.
I am emptiness without
dimension.

Ask me again, and I am
different, a changing portrait,
here then gone. I am what you
see and the invisible vessel
of divinity. Filled with
contradictions, I am also a
straight arrow aimed at truth.

The mystery and the end
of all dilemmas is as
near to me as the unseen
helix of my DNA. The
totality of all being is
inside me and also inside
you, because we share the
universal gospel of reality.

Tribute

The dogwood is gaining leaves
and losing flowers,
the balance clearly tipping now
from white to green.

Leafed limbs nod in tribute
to the petals as they fall,
endings and beginnings
nearly indistinguishable in the
heady exuberance of spring.

It Is Enough

It is enough right now
to taste one moment of
peace. Of course I want
more, but at least the
door is open.

It is enough to draw a
conscious breath and
let my hands relax,
fingers releasing their
tight grasp on things
outside of my control.

It is enough to shed a
layer of stress as if
taking off a jacket or a
pair of too-tight shoes.

Ease of being has to
start somewhere.
This breath is my
first step.

The Well of Emptiness

Beneath the bird calls and the
hiss of traffic, beneath my
heart beat and the even sound of
breathing, there is a well of
emptiness I often rush to fill.

Today, I let myself fall into it,
this bottomless expanse.
Terrifying, unifying, the
generative energy of nothing
harbors no judgment. Its utter
impersonality is stunning
to the mind, and I reach
reflexively for personality
to bind myself again to
something known.

It doesn't work though.
My ears ring with the silence
of the void. I hear the
stillness inside the ground
of being, the infinite
awareness that is completely
unmoved by my small fears
or my unique trajectory,
like the fading arc
of a shooting star
disappearing in the dark.

Dissolving Into Yes

Rest inside your perfect
wholeness, unassailed by
doubt. Rest within the
luminous moment of
knowing when the small
self disappears. Rest in
the remembering that
exists when all creation
is seen for what it is –
one free and conscious
being. We are, each one
of us, nothing but this,
our sense of separateness
dissolving into yes.

One Breath at a Time

Breathe with me in the
rhythm of mountain streams,
in the hypnotizing cadence
of waves breaking on
the shore. Breathe in the
peace that plays just beneath
the agitated surface of the
mind. Find the breath that
expresses your connection
to the silence, to abiding
forgiveness, to the shining
light of spirit in your heart.
Your own true breath can
release you from the prison
of your fears and plumb the
depths of your awareness.
It all starts here – the choice
to breathe, relax, and feel;
the choice to witness without
judgment, and allow the
truth of life to be revealed.

In the Moment
Before Choosing

In the moment before
choosing, every possibility
exists. Before the overlay
of self and separation is
choiceless, vast awareness.
I am, you are, we are that.

For one mind-stopping
instant I exist in this
unframed truth, and then
it slips from my hands
like beach sand.

This is what I have to say to you. The Mother of the Universe includes, includes, includes. She pushes away nothing and yet she remains the empty vessel, receptive, open, ready. This is her lesson – to be empty and overflowing, a blank canvas filled with light, a perfect poem unwritten, yet read within the heart. You too embody such paradoxes, the particular and the whole experiencing each moment.

The All includes absolute zero, the extinction of the personal, the impossible instant when the known blinks out and there are no points of reference left. This is the uncharted territory of the soul's journey, a step-by-step exploration and creation, both happening at once, the two acts actually one.

Embrace the World

May light be born anew
in me and you. May peace
reign within our hearts
and gratitude frame our
days with gladness and
with joy. May each one
of us awaken to the truth
and allow the universe
to use us, hearts, hands,
minds, and prayers, united
to embrace the world.

Source of My Despair

I seek to find the source of my despair,
and turn up only air. I'm certain there
must be some root cause to fix or shift –
a way I can be different – but no matter
where I look I find only the seamless
weave of infinity holding me close,
embracing me as if I am the prodigal
come home again. The truth is,
nothing's wrong. Moods rise and fall,
but underneath it all my essence is and
always has been whole and glorious.
I seek to find the source of my despair
and find instead the wide and silent
matrix of awareness.

Message to Myself

To this moment, as it is,
give in.

Allow reality to have its way,
to touch, and change,
and burn away
whatever still remains
of your illusions.

Now is knocking like the guest
who traveled a long distance
just to visit.
Would you keep her waiting
at the door?

Let life in, the beauty
and the contradictions,
the curriculum
perfectly designed
to pull the rug out from under
your favorite easy chair
before reducing it
to splinters.

Welcome in the tempest
and the calm,
opening the door for truth
no matter how
she finds you.

Receive the Wind

Receive the wind,
the howling wind, the
whistling, moaning,
keening wind. She
blows in without a
proper introduction,
cleans all corners of
their cobwebs, throws
the pine limbs into a
fine frenzy, disappears
with no farewell. Take
in the unstoppable
wildness, the ardent,
untamed strength.
Her great gusts don't
discriminate as she
sweeps away the
clutter of past seasons
with a spirited, fierce
grace.

What Self-Inquiry Reveals

When I listen very carefully
to the content of my mind,
I find this thought repeating
like a mantra: "Something's
wrong here," or at times it's
more pointed: "Something's
wrong with me." But self-
inquiry only reveals stillness,
the whole knowing itself in
infinite expression. Not once
has the great silence spoken
to me and said "You've
failed." It is I who point the
finger and cower in my shame.

Headlong Into Love

I slip into the swift river of grace
the moment I stop trying to control
my fate. The current takes my
breath away, leaving me amazed
at the release. Use me up, I say.
Smooth my rough edges
until I offer no resistance to the flow.

Within the enclosure of my open heart,
may awareness wake and take aim
at my last attempts to grasp the known.
I pray to give myself over to a strength
that isn't mine, to be carried by the
energy of change and evolution.

I pray to tumble headlong into love
and not reach out even once
to try and break the fall.

Raindrop

Today I am
a raindrop
on the surface
of the sea –
distinct but for
an instant, then
one with all
that is or ever
will be.

Every Possibility

Amid the thousand fears
that flesh is heir to, there
is also peace. When I
look beneath the boulder
of anxiety, the mountain
of my doubt, I find the
shining silence, and rest
until my being vibrates
with only one note.
This is what I bring into
my day, the wordless
sound of all creation,
the empty space of
every possibility poised
and ready to take shape.

Decree

As Abbot of this monastery
I decree a day of celebration.
Go find the peaks now hidden
in the clouds. Carouse and
dance, unfettered by coarse
robes or rope sandals. Take
the pages of rules by which
you've lived and toss them
like confetti in the wind.

Discipline and prayer have
taught that you are not the
doer of the deeds, but if you
know nothing about how to
proceed, what then?
Who are you without the
trappings of vocation?

I say leave behind the cold
stone hallways and run
barefoot in warm grass. Fall
in love with what is natural
and effortless. Dare to be
your whole, dear self,
riotously free, dancing like
no cloistered one can dance.
I say take and eat the feast
of your awakening.

Home Again

I slow my practice down,
breathing as the ocean
breathes, flowing easily
from pose to pose, not
knowing what comes
next. Energy streams
through as I let go of
everything I've learned
or seen. I follow where
this life force leads –
holding, loosening,
sinking into stillness
and then moving on,
but only when the time
is ripe. I slow down to
find heart and mind
already aligned with
body. Savoring each
sensation, I come home
again to my own sweet
peace, to the depth and
mystery of this release.

In the Name of Your Awakening

A voice spoke as I roused
myself from sleep:
"The path to peace is not
serene. It will use you up
and bring the whole of
you forward into light.
If you don't wish to be
seen in your entirety, go
back to sleep right now.
If you desire to be known
clear through, deeper
even than bone, I bid you
rise. Greet the day with
gladness and choose not
to label anything that
comes your way as
blessing or misfortune.
This I say in the name
of your awakening."

Self-Acceptance

In the midst of difficulty,
my curiosity is piqued
and I aim the lance of
self-inquiry into the
center of my deepest fears.

I give myself permission
to feel exactly what I feel,
to be just as I am, and in
that self-acceptance I find
energy, awareness, and a
thousand gifts I never
guessed were with me
all along.

Lineage

Lineage is a line through time
connecting potent symbols
of the past with present practice.
Heritage gives us riverbanks
to contain energy, rules to follow
then toss aside, boundaries to
break through, and finally
the discernment to find truth
wherever it might hide.

Lineage is only as alive as those
who walk its paths just long
enough to grow strong, but not
so long that dogma becomes
a closed casket, or belief resists
officiating at its own funeral.

There Will Be Spring

Fall is at its most
exuberant today.
I point to an
exquisite maple,
leaves like orange
flame and say,
When I go, I want
it to be that way –
a blaze of glory,
nothing held back.
I want to celebrate
until the last leaf
blows off my last
bare branch and
trust that of course
there will be Spring.

This is what I have to say to you. Allow your mind to quiet just a bit. It has been spiraling inward, obsessing on small details of future events. Stuck in an endless loop of worry, it chews on its own tail. Take a moment with your eyes closed and try this experiment.

Invite the spiral to turn upward. Imagine the mind opening to receive the wisdom of the universe, innate goodness, the energy to remember that only this moment has potency. What is past or yet to come cannot be directly experienced, but this moment can.

Be as intimate with your next breath as you wish to be with truth. Experience every nuance of being alive in this body, at this time, with these thoughts, emotions, fears, and doubts. Be here and nowhere else, and trust that you don't need to worry in order for events to play out as they will. You don't need to stay tense to function well. In fact, exactly the reverse is true.

Let go of grasping, and in that momentary relaxation, creativity comes alive and problems you can never solve with mind come clear through intuition and the vast intelligence of truth.

Winds of Change

The winds of change
rattle windows in their
frames and bend tree
trunks like grass blades.
I cannot dodge the
raindrops pelting helter-
skelter on my face.
The tempest will find
my sanctuary and beat
upon the door as if the
gods themselves are
restless, hell-bent on
my transformation.

Despite sound so loud
I can barely think, I
unbolt the door, open
it wide, knowing with
a certainty beyond
mind that not even
this fierce storm can
alter the unchanging
truth of what I am.
There is a still point
wind can't reach, fire
can't burn, flood can't
drown. An ax can't
cleave in two what is
and always has been
whole and true.

First Frost

First frost exhales its white breath,
the kiss of death to tender summer
blooms. It rakes its frigid fingers
across the lawn, under the scarlet
dogwood leaves, over the doomed,
unopened buds of morning glories.
First frost silences the crickets and
lays its chill hand in blessing upon
the earth as the season turns and
mountains blaze with light.

Explosion of Unknowing

The whole open-ended
miracle of life is right
here inside this breath.
The journey from unreal
to real lives here in this
present moment explosion
of unknowing. I can try
to make it match some
expectation, but it's all
right here, the door to
truth flung wide.

Cast Aside the Costume

It is time to cast aside
the costume of identity,
the mask, the too tight
pants, the classy silk
blouse that says "I am
someone" to the world.
My heart is pounding
loudly in my ears. My
hands are clammy.
Unclothed and awake
I long to slip inside a
new identity, tie it like
a robe around my waist,
retreat to a place where
the layout is familiar.

I want to contain the
fear, print a business
card explaining who
I am, but instead, as
an experiment, I dance.
I unleash the energy of
movement, laughter,
anger, passion, prayer.
It's all there, creativity
tangled in my wild hair,
and I am free, a whirl
of naked limbs, one with
everything that is. My
eyes and mind and spirit
open wide. Just think of it –
I've spent my whole life
trying to avoid this.

Praise or Longing

Oh holiest of holies, I pray
for the molecules of me to be
reconstituted, new, inseparably
part of you. I pray to radiate at the
same wave length as the beating
of your heart; to see as you see,
to hear with your ears, to feel the
texture of truth as you do. May I
dissolve into you, free at last to
know every word I've written or
uttered in the past as either
praise or longing.

Empty

Empty as a frame
without a painting,
bare as slate exposed
by wind and rain –
only when I am
empty can I then
be filled with truth.

One Embrace

I breathe in blessings,
bird song, the light of
stars dimming in the
dawn. I breathe in
mystery and mountain
streams, equanimity
and the audacity to live
boldly, freely, willingly
in service to the whole.
My open hands rest
lightly on my knees.
They vibrate with energy,
fill with possibility and
grace. I breathe out
judgment, expectations,
doubt, and everything
that handcuffs me
and holds me back.
Breath completes the
circle of ebb and flow,
highs and lows, form
and formless joined
in one embrace.

Rogue Mind

Come back, you rogue
mind, determined to find
the cloud behind every
silver lining. You flit
hither and yon, never
asking my permission,
rarely sitting still. You
delight in adding items
to your litany of concerns.
Rest here in contentment?
That's boring, you say.
There's a war to be fought
with reality today! There
are lists to be made, mistakes
to point out, a brisk trade
in guilt and shame to engage
in. I've only found one sure
way to tame your wild nature.
If I ask, "Who are you," you
slow down to chew on this
conundrum. When I say
"Tell me what is true," you
focus like a searchlight,
illumined, and intent.
Finally we work as one,
mind and soul and heart
combined and reveling
in truth.

Whole and Weightless

In the moments before sleep
there is an instant when
surrender is complete.

From behind closed eyes, I see
the emptiness and do not retreat.
I hear the great silence and do not
rush to fill it.

The void equalizes so that what is
inside me, peering out, and
what is outside – at long last
both are recognized as one.

I nearly weep at this revelation,
as if nothing and everything meet
at the boundary of sleep and
all the stories I've told myself
now fall away to leave me
whole and weightless.

Hologram

I give you a handful
of leaves, these spent
nurturers of trees now
brown and dry as dust.
I give you the wing
feather of a raven, blue-
black and iridescent.
I give you a stone so
polished by the ocean
that I'm sure you can
see your true face
reflected in its surface.
With these gifts of
earth and sky and sea,
with these small bits
of the infinite, you can
know the whole. One
blade of grass reveals
the secrets of meadow,
prairie, and savannah.
One breath drawn in
with awareness awakens
every corner of the soul.

Cradle of Awakening

Unto you is born all possibility.
Receive this sky-clad babe,
this seed of being, this spark of
light in darkness. Hear the angel
choir sing, "Glory be to God on
high." Look into the child's eyes
and dive so deep within that pool
of love that you finally believe in
your own goodness. Don't give up
on yourself, even when the days
are at their darkest, for the mysterious
star is shining again in the East,
beckoning you to the cradle of
awakening, calling you to peace.

Flower of Truth

Let the subtle flow
of energy lead.
Be the freedom and
magnificence you
believed could only
be achieved through
years of struggle.

Allow the movement
and the moment to
unfold you petal by
petal until you are
wide open – the
flower of truth in
unselfconscious
full bloom.

Praise to the Creator

Praise to the creator of these
snowflakes. Praise to the One
who fashioned seasons out of
nothing, cardinals out of dust,
oak trees out of water, rock,
and primal wonder. Praise to the
spinner of dreams, the conjurer
who put green into grass, heat
in summer, raised mountains
from the flatlands. Praise to the
invisible things, to air and energy,
and sound waves coalescing
into symphonies. Praise to the
giver of gifts and that which
takes our last breath back into
vastness, mixing it with love
and starstuff so we too are
infinite, nothing truly lost
in the transition.

Ecstasy Lives

Ecstasy exists. It lives in
random acts of love, bird
seed scattered on cold days,
back rubs, words of praise
or admiration. It lives within
the spontaneous admission
of defeat when things don't
go as planned. Ecstasy lies
dormant, ready to burst forth
when a whitetail deer leaps
across the road, or a slice of
waning moon hangs jewel-like
in the night. It's easy to miss,
simpler to point toward
suffering and shrug, choose
not to hear that first ecstatic
call of a mourning dove
welcoming the sunrise.

Truth Leads

Open and focused, I am present
to inner quiet and the sensory
explosion of the day. This doesn't
mean that my mind never runs away
with me, but the universe is shot
through with truth like gold thread
lighting up plain fabric.

No matter where I look, it's there –
a flash of knowing, a moment
of repose. Surrendering to
this guidance, truth leads me
not away from engagement,
but straight into
the fiery heart of life.

Peace Be With You

Peace be with you even in
uncertainty and change.
The peace that enters with
each breath also descends
from all directions.

The east brings hope,
the west opens up the door
for dreams. The north and
south will reveal their secrets
in due time.

The mountains and the
solid ground beneath your feet
both offer peace.

The whispered voice of truth
refuses to believe in any
reality that isn't rooted in
peace of mind and heart.

Peace be with you, in doing
and in rest, now and always,
                    Amen.

This is what I have to say to you. It is possible to be whole, to hold the space for the personal witness, the Beloved, the world, and the vastness all at once, to express the formed and formless. Of course this is way too big for the mind to grasp, let alone control. And of course it seems impossible. But this is what awakening is – allowing the impossible to live and be and breathe within your being, which isn't you at all, in the small and personal sense. The whole is everywhere. The emptiness is you and me and every grain of sand and mote of dust.

Truth isn't concerned whether your small self quakes before enormity. Anxiety doesn't change truth and can't even make you smaller unless you let it. Live the truth of your awakening today, the infinite and the particular integrated through and through, the Source coming alive in your eyes, your smile, your heart opening wider and wider until love knows no boundaries at all, and the universe is happening in you.

Index of Titles and First Lines

About the Author

Danna Faulds writes all her poems longhand in lined notebooks, pausing during her morning yoga practice, or sitting for a few minutes after meditation. A former librarian, Danna works part-time as an archivist at the Woodrow Wilson Presidential Library, does free-lance editing for Kripalu Center, and occasionally teaches writing workshops. She lives with her husband, Richard, in the Shenandoah Valley of Virginia where they try to keep one step ahead of the weeds in their organic vegetable garden and enjoy the wildlife on their rural property.

Danna is a practitioner and teacher of Kripalu Yoga. She writes about her practice:

The potent combination of meditation, yoga, and writing has brought lasting transformation into my life. I can't point to any one practice and say it's responsible, but together they have shifted just about everything about me.

The transformative process isn't always blissful. In fact, it is often profoundly uncomfortable, but when it really comes down to it, what else is there? Yoga and meditation fuel the fire, and writing gives me a way to read the smoke signals that rise up from inner experience. I take delight in reporting on the journey.

Danna can be reached by e-mail at yogapoems@aol.com